The Voice of Their Hearts

Learning Animal Communication

Shirl Knobloch

• • •

The Voice of Their Hearts: Learning Animal Communication

© Shirley Knobloch, 2017

All rights reserved

Edited by: Jennifer Sabatelli

Cover, Artwork, and Photography by: Shirl Knobloch

ISBN 13: 978-0-9974752-8-9

• • •

Also By Shirl Knobloch:

Birdsong, Barks, and Banter: Adventures of an Animal Intuitive Reiki Master and Her Home of Misfit Companions

The Returning Ones: A Medium's Memoirs

You're Never Too Old for Fairy Tales

Reenactments from My Heart: Spiritual and Supernatural Civil War Fiction and Poetry

Once Upon a Fairy Tale

Strength of a Lion, Soul of a Lamb: A Collection of Wolfhound Fairy Tales and Poetry

My Ten Legged Journey: The Road to Rainbow Bridge

Waiting for the Next Village Attack: Growing Up Italian, a Jersey Girl Reminisces

Enchanted: Fairy Tales for Old and Young

● ● ●

Dedicated to each beautiful soul with whom my heart has had the privilege to communicate over the years

• • •

...

Table of Contents

Prologue	1
Can I Learn to Be an Animal Communicator?	3
Layers	7
What Do Most Animals Communicate?	15
Communicating with Those Abused	17
Do Animals Know When Death Is Near?	19
Do I Believe in the Rainbow Bridge?	21
Beginning	23
My Perceptions of Animal and Human Energy	25
Animal Chakras	31
Colors and Animals	35
Getting to Know Them	45
Practicing Animal Communication	49
Pet Auras	55
Is Animal Communication Dangerous?	57
Learning Meditation	59
Practicing with Friends	65

• • •

Building Your Confidence	67
Personalities	69
Do Pets Come Back?	71
Epilogue	73
Review	75
Space for Personal Journal Entries	77

Prologue

Many years ago, I had my own Reiki practice, specializing in the care of animals using Reiki energy. I sometimes held workshops in animal Reiki and animal communication. Now, almost a decade later, I still receive requests from those interested in learning to be a communicator. I have held internet communication sessions all around the globe, from Australia to South Africa, England, and the U.S. For all who wish they were close enough to travel to one of my animal communication workshops, I wrote this book for you to learn and practice in the privacy and comfort of your own home, with the ones dear to your hearts.

I thought it was time to pen my experiences and teachings. Although every individual's results will be unique, I welcome hearing from all of you. Please write a short note on my book page if this book is helpful to you.

Thanks,
Shirl

Can I Learn to Be an Animal Communicator?

Everyone has special psychic gifts. All are strong in childhood; most are tossed by the wayside when the struggles and stress of adult life overshadow childhood imaginations. Think back to your own childhood. Did you have an intense interest in communicating with animals and the unseen world? I did.

When I was very young, I would stick my neck out of my bedroom window and sing to the birds. I stopped when a nosey neighbor told me she heard me. I was too embarrassed to continue. I read a memorable story in *Ripley's Believe It or Not* when I was about eight years old. (I loved *Ripley's*; I always associated with the misfits, never feeling like I belonged within the lines of black and white myself. I work as an artist now, often using charcoals. Perhaps I love charcoals because they blend the blackness with the light so beautifully. To get back to *Ripley's*, though...) The story was about a young girl in England who could call the birds to her shoulders. I wanted to be that girl. The gift faded as she grew. Most of our gifts do. The secret is to bring them up from the dark regions of our soul and subconscious, where they lay waiting to be unwrapped.

When I taught animal communication to students at my office, I could usually tell who would venture further in exploration of this ability. There would be the smiling young women who came in gushing that they loved animals. Then, there would be the quiet, introverted woman who sat in the back of the class, intensely observing. That was the one. As I have said many times, it is the tortured soul who seeks out animals, the soul who has been hurt in life by fellow humans. It is that soul who turns its heart's trust to the innocents of the world who have also been abandoned, hurt, and betrayed. It is this group who become the communicators, not the happy Dr. Doolittle "wannabes." Those of us whose hearts want to connect with animals in a profound way will become the communicators.

Reaching into a troubled animal's heart is not easy. There will be suffering, grief, and sorrow. But there will also be an energy more loving, trusting, and forgiving than one has ever known.

For those of us who never quite fit in, for those of us who were bullied, envied, feared, and misunderstood for gifts we were too young to understand...this is the common denominator that binds us together. Animals have been the constant friend to those broken souls.

Layers

Our souls are like the Grand Canyon. Have you ever gazed at the Grand Canyon in photographs and seen the layers of the earth's crust? You can separate the periods of history by looking at the layers in the rock. I believe our souls are like those layers, each layer like a past life and our current life's memories, each one sculpting who we have become. As an intuitive, I have been fortunate to glimpse layers of my past, layers that have formed in previous centuries. I have written about these in earlier books, so I will not go into depth here. But these layers have a common thread—they have been filled with sorrow.

My life started out in sorrow. I was bullied every day as a child. I remember the words, I remember running home crying. It is in those formative years when betrayal by humans forms a layer of sorrow around one's heart and soul's crust. Children in kindergarten learned the art of name calling quite proficiently and improved upon that skill through all my years of schooling. My Roman nose was the target and, combined with my intelligence, made for the slogan, "the nose knows" (their favorite, although not the meanest in their repertoire of hurt).

When I was 8 years old, my grandpa died. My grandma was in her 80s and spoke no English. Now, as an adult, I realize she must have loved me, but back then, she was a scary old woman in black. I had a huge double bed in my room. It was my oasis. I loved that bed. Already several years into the name-calling that started in kindergarten, my room was my sanctuary. I went to school, came home, and read fairy tales on my bed in my room. I had no human friends. I had no pets; I wasn't allowed any as a child. Soon after my grandpa died, my mother asked if I would share my bed and room with my grandma. I was horrified at this thought, sharing a room and bed with this scary woman who spoke no words I could understand. I said no. Six weeks later, she died.

My adult brain can now comprehend that grief propelled my mother to speak a few words to me that would change that layer in my life forever. She yelled that it was my fault. Just four words can mold a heart. I still carry those words in my heart. When a pet dies, my heart whispers them to me. It was my fault. Did I do enough? Did I choose the right treatment? Did I feed the right food?

Soon after my grandma died, a big Goodwill or Salvation Army truck pulled up to our door. Moving men entered my room and took that huge bed away. I got a small twin frame that had been stored away in our attic. My mother told my dad that I needed more space in my room. I didn't say a word. I knew the reason.

I think that event was the first catalyst in my life of saving all those that others deemed beyond salvation...the misfits, the blind, the old, the ones too scary to love. I loved them all. My mother was a good mother; she never meant to hurt me. But in her time of deepest grief, she released some of it onto a child too young to understand. Losing both of her parents just weeks apart was too much for her to bear. My adult mind sees how that overwhelmed her soul. I understand now. I understand how we hurt those we love most in life without meaning to, and I understand how each one of those hurts shapes us into the beings we become.

These childhood hurts lay deep within our soul's crust. As time passes, this crust shifts and moves; the focus of life changes. Living continues, and we aren't the little children being called names on the playground anymore. But those soul layers in our life crust, like the earth's seismic plates, continue to shift and touch each other every so often.

Something as simple as a memory, a news story, or a dream can bring them to the surface again, and that crack in our crust can become a tsunami of grief.

In those times of grief, animals have always been the ones I could depend on, the ones that never hurt my heart. As I graduated school and started my path in life, I realized I could have done things to alter my appearance, make myself more part of what is normally accepted. It would have straightened the bump in my nose, but those wounds could never be smoothed. They are part of me, part of who I am, the reason I have formed such bonds with those that are not accepted as capable of communication.

But they do communicate. Animals love, they grieve, they hurt, they remember, and most of all, they forgive unconditionally. When betrayal by those who are supposed to heal your heart, not break it, manifests, a deeper trust in animals ensues. And when animals sense a heart that has been broken, they instinctively reach out to heal those wounds. That is why therapy animals provide such a service to those whose souls and bodies are not the accepted "norm." To an animal's heart, there is no disability or deformity. There is only kindness, and when that kindness is returned, deep love forms. It is this deeper connection that makes communication possible.

When one's heart understands the depths of sorrow and betrayal, it can recognize and acknowledge this in other beings. This is animal communication. I share these memories to shed light on how one journeys into the world of animal communication. Gifts develop when hurt from humans creates a longing to connect with those who only break hearts when they must leave. I am not saying that deep hurt must forge the path for every animal communicator; however, I am saying it often does.

Animals have the most loving energy I have encountered. But like us, some have layers and scars. Some of those layers are too hard to overcome and result in animals that can turn in a matter of moments. Few instances of pets-turning-on-humans involve animals raised from infancy. In most cases where a pet turns on a family member, the pet was a rescue or an adoptee with an unknown past. But any animal can turn, just as any human can. We have yet to understand all the mysteries and ailments of both the human and animal brain.

First and foremost, before you begin to venture out doing any type of animal work, keep safety and precaution in your mind. When I was just beginning to schedule animal communication sessions, I went to the home of a woman who told me she had a very gentle and friendly dog. I learned I could fly that day. Her chow lunged at me to bite and threw me against the wall. She told me he had never done anything like this before since the time she adopted him, which was only a few days earlier. Frankly, she did not know this dog. I have often wondered what ensued, as she told me he was a favorite with the little kids in the neighborhood. Perhaps he was a friend to the children. Perhaps a woman, not a child, had left a layer upon his heart. (Years later, another woman called and said her chow needed Reiki. She wasn't very friendly, she added, so maybe I could just sit on one side of the room and do it distantly. Of course, I was apprehensive. It turns out that this chow was one of my most cherished clients. She would fall asleep in my arms, never once a peep out of her lion-like head.)

Another time, my husband brought home a shepherd from a rescue where a co-worker volunteered. The dog loved my husband and my kids but hated me. I would pass by her while she was resting and see her lips snarl up at the corner. She actually did bite the palm of my hand, and still I did not give up on her. Finally, though, with the advice of a vet, we returned her to the shelter. This dog had snarled at the vet when he reached to examine her mouth and ears. He told me I had a ticking bomb in my home that could explode at me any moment. I might pick up a broom, a mop...who knows what tool of abuse was used against this girl? Her next home's feline resident didn't fare as well as I did. My husband's co-worker later confessed that the shepherd had lived with a petite, longhaired brunette who abused her. Petite, longhaired—that description fit me very accurately. Though sorrowful, I made the right decision in giving her back to the shelter, instead of waiting for the day I made an all-too-familiar move that opened up a layer in her heart. As I wrote in the beginning of this chapter, some layers are hard to peel away; they leave sticky residue, like faded roses blooming on torn wall papered walls.

If you wish to become an animal intuitive, learn as much about animal behavior as you can from experienced trainers and animal behaviorists, and make sure you get as much information from pet guardians about the history of their pets (including how long they have lived with said pets). When you begin conducting sessions with unfamiliar animals, you need not communicate hands on. Sit across the room, give each other space, and make friends before you try to access confidences held inside them. You may also use photographs if you feel comfortable doing so. Energy travels without boundaries; I can affect the energy of a pet with distant Reiki or intuitive communication even if an ocean separates the two of us.

What Do Most Animals Communicate?

All of the animals I have communicated with share one common thread. Foremost in their hearts is letting the ones who loved them know that their love and kindness was reciprocated. Many ask if their dogs blamed them for euthanasia. This I equate to humans asking if their family members forgave them after crossing into spirit. There is no blame, only love. The only thing they wish is for the ones left behind to be at peace.

Some pets do come for visits. Some refuse to leave if the one they love cannot find peace and acceptance. Most pets who are still alive only wish more time from busy guardians or more attention if they feel another new family member has displaced them.

One very poignant German shepherd kept showing me a cemetery. After she crossed, her grieving owner confessed that after her husband died, she could never bear to visit his grave. She told me that after her dog crossed, she finally went to visit her husband's resting place in the cemetery. This incredible dog, while alive, tried to give her that peace, wanting her to visit that gravesite. Each time I told this woman of the dog's message, she said it made no sense to her. To me, it made perfect sense; this woman's peace was so important to her dog that she tried repeatedly to tell me in order for her mom to hear. When this woman confided her cemetery visit to me, I knew what a treasure this dog had been and why her mom carried her heavy body up the flight of steps to my Reiki office each week to visit when she no longer could walk on her own. Dogs live for our happiness, and the greatest gift we can give them in death is continuing on, to give happiness and love to another.

Communicating with Those Abused

I often do sessions on newly adopted pets. These beings carry baggage, just as humans carry baggage upon their souls. The one difference is that these animals never speak of anger; they speak of pain, they speak of fear, but they never speak of rage. Their hearts forgive and trust us again, even after the most horrendous beginnings.

Of course, there are exceptions. There are some so troubled they are unreachable. If your path ever intersects with one of these troubled souls, don't blame yourself as a failure if you cannot save them. Some animals cannot be saved, just as some people cannot be saved. Sometimes, the trauma or the imbalance in a being can never be rehabilitated. It is a hard lesson you will learn when you devote your life to helping them. I know—there have been a couple I could not save. I could only love.

Do Animals Know When Death Is Near?

In my years of animal communication, I have felt evidence (many times over) that animals do indeed know when death is coming. In fact, the study of primates in the wild has brought footage to light of elderly members of particular groups walking off on their own........to die.

I remember a beautiful, black cat that came to my office. He was skin and bones; anyone could realize his time was approaching. I felt his time was very, very near. Looking into the desperate eyes of the woman who loved him, I said nothing. I don't share thoughts such as these, for the guardians will know soon enough; another day of blind hope is something I would never deny. I did Reiki on this cat. I felt his energy close to crossing. A couple of days later, she stopped me in the hallway of my office (we shared the same building). She said someone had left the door open at home and her cat was now missing. He had never once shown any interest in venturing outside. They searched and searched to no avail. I knew he had wandered off like that elderly primate member, wanting to spare the rest of his family the pain of his crossing.

That is such a testament to devotion. She never found his body, but I hope he found the beautiful spot he so deserved to take his final mortal breaths.

Animals have that same sense about people. There is the extraordinary nursing home cat that always chooses the right bed upon which to share final hours. How do they know when we, humans, are in pain, in mourning, or about to cross? There is a tremendous energy connection between humans and our pets. They sense changes in energy, both within themselves and within us. Once you start to read auras, your senses will heighten, but never to the extent of those with whom we share our hearts and homes. As we advanced technologically as a race, we lost some primal gifts along the way. It is my hope that one day they will once again exist within each of us.

Do I Believe in the Rainbow Bridge?

This is the question I am asked most often. Those in grief want to believe. They look and listen for signs constantly—a feather, a bark, the touch of a spirit paw.

I genuinely believe that energies don't die. I have journaled too many of my own personal experiences (and received notes from others about their own) not to believe. Is there a Rainbow Bridge or a heavenly Elysian Field? No spirit has ever communicated to me a thought or picture of either, but what I do believe and feel is energy. The energy leaves one realm and enters another. I have felt it leave in animals I held in my arms as they were dying. I have felt it during communication sessions. The energy of a living being is different from the energy of one who has crossed. Though different, it is just as powerful a force. It is a force of love, protection, and guardianship, one that does not perish when flesh, fur, and bones do. Scientists brush this off as imaginings of a brain in crisis. I believe it is the spark of new life just beginning in our energetic being.

Beginning

If you have serious interest in animal communication, you should start first by learning about mortal energy. By this, I mean investigating a tai chi, yoga, or Reiki class. By accepting that our bodies seem physical but are indeed so much more, you can begin to accept that all energy on earth is connected. Invisible tracks of energy can send thoughts to and from givers and recipients. Some pick up these tracks of energy in the form of pictures. Some pick them up as emotions; these individuals are the empaths of the world. Some pick them up as words. I once wrote that receiving words from animals is a lot like reading—you hear the words in your head, but you don't really hear them. Rather, you acknowledge or understand them.

As I said before, everyone has abilities. Every person can make a drawing if handed a crayon. Some drawings will be better than others. But better is a challenging word. Some might be more colorful, some might be more precisely detailed, but each has some endearing quality. And so it is with humans and their intuitive abilities. Taking an energy class will amplify whatever qualities you already possess.

They are inside those layers, waiting to be peeled away. When you first venture into the field of animal communication, you will soon see your strengths begin to take form. Do you hear words? Do you see pictures? Do you feel the emotions of animals? Perhaps all three.

My Perceptions of Animal and Human Energy

(You can go to any internet site, type in "chakras" or "energy centers," and lists of web pages will come up in search feeds. I will touch upon some here, but for further study, you can find this information easily online.)

Human energy centers (or chakras) and animal energy centers (or chakras) are very similar. However, animals have retained sensitivity on many more areas of their bodies than we have. No wonder touching an animal's paws or ears or whiskers can be too much for some pets. It would be like you hitting your funny bone against the doorframe......stars of energy.

Humans have seven main energy centers. Each corresponds to balance of the physical body, each has a color or colors associated with it, and each has emotions linked to its spin. Starting from the ground upward, we first have the root chakra. This is the energy of the trunk and legs of our body. People who feel stuck in life sometimes manifest an imbalance in their leg and foot energy, which can manifest in all sorts of symptoms. Lower back pain also resides within this region, as well as issues of the lower bowel. This root chakra holds our fears, our primal fears. It is also a source of being grounded, which I will discuss further in the book.

Imbalance in any chakra means the energy is too weak or too strong. Here, color therapy is beneficial. The earth colors pertain to this chakra. From deep reds and russets to browns and blacks, these colors are the ones we focus on in the root chakra area. Too dominant an energy, one should shy away from wearing red. When looking to be grounded or be protected, wearing black is the best option.

Next is the sacral chakra, or the energy center of our reproductive organs. Although the imbalance may very well be affecting our physical system, the idea of creativity or purpose in life is centered within this location, too. This is an area where women sometimes face problems around mid-life, when goals and purpose are questioned.

This is an area very pertinent in my own personal quest to learn about Reiki and the energy of our body. In my forties, I was working two very stressful jobs. I was helping manage a construction office and working as a realtor. One day at my desk, it was as if someone just flicked a switch—I started hemorrhaging very badly. It was then that my whole path in life changed. I studied energy and stress and its correlation and subsequently opened my own Reiki practice. I also began writing, something that I always held as a dream for "one day."

One does not have to be in mid life to be affected in this area. Many young women have troublesome symptoms that might be due to some emotional as well as physical imbalance (since all of our energies are linked). The colors of fiery oranges to bright reds signify this energy. If one doesn't "light a fire" under his/her goals in life, the flames of passion extinguish, leaving a trail of smoke that can slowly suffocate his/her well-being.

Next is the solar plexis chakra. This is our gut. I am sure you have heard of gut instinct; this is the area referred to by these words. If something doesn't feel right in your gut, it usually isn't. Maybe those butterflies or stomachaches are telling you to change course. Many believe our very souls are tied to our physical bodies by a silver cord attached to this area. When that cord is detached, our soul is free to fly. Anger is stored here, hence ulcers erupt in people who store negativity in this region. It is a center of ego and self-confidence; too little or too much is equally bad. The color yellow is associated here. If you want to convey confidence and a sunny self-esteem without the dominance of a fiery red, wear yellow to get your point across. (It is no wonder that so many restaurants and chains use red and yellow in their logos, appealing to our hungry stomachs.)

The next is the very important heart chakra. You will open this chakra to both receive animal communication and transfer communication to animals. Its color is pink, thought to be the most gentle color to soothe man and animal alike. That is why so many mental facilities and even prisons use pink in their environments; pink is a calming shade. The color green may also be used in working with the heart chakra. Jade is highly revered in Asian cultures as the healing stone. Grief is stored in this chakra. When I read auras, I certainly pick up on the heavy emotion of grief. Lung issues are found here; smokers' auras tell their stories.

Next is the throat chakra, very important in verbal communication. Our animal communication is more of the heart kind, but if you work in a field where communication plays a vital role, keep this area balanced. Blue is the dominant color here. Wear a blue scarf on the day of your business presentation. Issues with the throat, teeth, or jaw are pertinent here. I once read the aura of a woman where I asked if she suffered from TMJ. Her astounded eyes accompanied her revelatory words; her dentist told her *that very afternoon* that she had this issue! Allergies also reside here, as well as sinus issues. Emotional trauma from verbal abuse may also be harbored here.

Next up is the chakra with which most of us are familiar: our third eye chakra. This chakra is linked to our vision, meaning sight, as well as vision of another kind—our psychic vision (which will be utilized in animal communication work). If you suffer from migraines, this is the chakra in need of alignment. I can always tell a "busy head," by that I mean a person with endless thoughts. Their third eye chakra is always buzzing. The color here can range from a light violet to a deep indigo, depending on how advanced this chakra is.

Finally, we have the crown chakra. This is the opposite of the root chakra. Both are extremely important when doing any kind of psychic work. A root chakra too dominant can result in depression; a crown chakra too dominant can result in a detachment from reality. Keep these two balanced by engaging in meditation exercises, one of which I will detail later. The crown chakra is the white divine light, like that of a quartz crystal (which is the king of all crystals in the mineral world).

Animal Chakras

Animals have a root chakra as well. Hip dysplasia, anal sac ailments, and leg tumors are all physical manifestations that correlate to this chakra. Many believe this is the chakra that pertains to barking; dogs may bark out of fear or dominance, hence the root chakra is associated with this behavior.

If a dog is being spayed or neutered, or has a tumor in the reproductive region, focus on the sacral chakra.

Digestive issues or sensitive stomachs will have the solar plexus as the target region.

Dogs endure grief, thus their heart chakras can be deeply affected by the loss of a sibling or guardian. Heart and lung issues are focused here.

Dogs sensitive to allergies or plagued with thyroid issues will need their throat chakras aligned. If undergoing a dental procedure, focus here as well.

Vision problems (such as cataracts) are associated with the third eye region, as well as any neurological or seizure disorders.

Animals are extremely intuitive; this chakra region is well tuned for their protection. Why is it that some pets don't like certain people and some pets naturally gravitate toward others? In some cases, animals sense a person is afraid of them and will try to approach this individual to warm his/her reluctant heart. Prey animal senses are keen; their intuitive chakra helps them sense danger (aside from or in addition to seeing, smelling, or hearing it). They are empathic beings, despite what skeptics may say, and feel grief and love for fellow animals and human caregivers.

At the very top is the crown chakra, our connection with all the divine energy surrounding us. Animals have been witnessed in moments of what can only be described as prayer. Chimpanzees have been seen to throw rocks into a great waterfall, in what animal behaviorists describe as primitive offerings.

This is just a brief overview. As I wrote earlier, there are countless articles, easily accessible, with information about all chakra centers. One important thing to note: chakra work is in no way a substitute for medical intervention. It is a complementary aid to soothe and balance.

Colors and Animals

If your dog is an alpha, stay away from red collars, leashes, and blankets. (The same also applies to children. If you have a hyperactive child, don't place a red blanket on his/her bed. You want a soothing color to calm down, not fire up what already burns too brilliantly.) Choose items that are light blue or green for a male dog or a soothing pink for a female. Likewise, steer away from the color red for noisy barkers. On the contrary, if you have a submissive dog, always on his back and letting others in the pack take advantage, buy him that red collar or bed; give him some confidence. Bright yellow or orange can work well, too.

Talking with Bram

Sharing a Laugh with Casper

Conversing with a Reindeer

Val and I

My Beautiful Boy, Now Living On in Spirit

Even Squirrels Have Voices in Their Hearts

Canary Chat

Chatting with Tiger Lily, My Bunny

Group Discussion

Everyone Joining in the Conversation

My Special Little Guy

Getting to Know Them

It takes years of living with multiple animals to get to know their energies and personalities. Only from living among them can you see the unique differences that make each one his/her own little furry being. You learn that they are capable of empathy, jealousy, and spitefulness, just like non-furry creatures (people).

I have been among so many who have been ill and have crossed that I now have a sense when that time is coming. My vet has told me on numerous occasions, "You always seem to know." Yes, if one works with energy, one can feel a difference in the energy field as well as see the changes in each personality.

I have held many in my arms as the time for crossing neared. I can best explain it as a feeling of one energy leaving and joining another. You can feel the release around them as their own energy field mingles with all the energies around us...seen and unseen.

If you live your life with many animals, you will see the subtle changes when life is at its end. They will hide it as best as they can, for as long as they can, for our sake. But you will see the fear in their glance and the dimming of sparkle from their eyes.

I don't communicate with my own pets. In times of illness, they let me know. There have been times when the vet took light of a situation that I knew was far more serious, and as it turned out, I was right. They also let me know, as I said before, when it is the time to leave me. Many people have the impression that I sit all day and talk to my pets. Yes, I talk to them, but just like you do. I love them just like you do. (As a side note, I don't do readings on my family members either. I have learned throughout my lifetime that each individual has to live his/her own mistakes and learn his/her own lessons. The few times I have tried to intervene did not turn out well. Others don't listen anyway.)

Once you begin to explore the world of animal communication and subscribe to the belief that energy connects all of us, your entire life will shift. The suffering of innocent animals will have greater weight on your heart. Ours is a world that will not soon turn away from the marketing and farming of animals as a food supply. Let your heart find its compassion, whether it be through a routine blessing over your meals, the purchase of humanely-raised meat, or the conviction to avoid consumption of products connected to animal suffering entirely. Your heart will have compassion for all around you— the oceans, the trees, and the planet upon which you walk. We are all connected beings, each with our own energy field.

Practicing Animal Communication

To start, it is probably best to choose and use a photo of your pet. Your pet will detect any anxiety in your energy field as you make first attempts at communication, so I feel a photo helps both of you in the beginning. As you become more confident, you can sit with your pet. Just don't choose a time when your pet wants to play or eat, or is agitated by a storm or noise coming from outside. During a storm is not the best time to ask your pet why he starts shaking.

In the next chapter, I will give an exercise to do beforehand, but this chapter will give you a general idea of what to expect.

First, you have to clear your thoughts. This sounds easy, but it isn't. The photo will help your concentration. I want you to gaze at the photo and, with a clear mind, see what enters. It is the first thoughts that matter. Take notice of the first thoughts. You can sit there thinking of twenty other thoughts, but I promise you that nineteen of them will only be figments of your imagination. This exercise is intended for you to receive the energy from *their* minds, not yours.

When you become confident enough for a personal chat, make sure only one pet is in the room. Bring the client into your bedroom and close the door. Give the others (if there are any) a treat to make them feel less left out and focus on just the one beside you.

You can ask a question if you like or just ask the pet to communicate what he/she wishes to tell you. My sessions are done this way. I don't promise answers to questions, but sometimes, if it is an important issue, information will flow through. I remember the time a woman asked why her son's dog was acting in a negative way. I told her the dog wasn't feeling as if her son was spending enough time with him. Sure enough, her son was renovating a new home and had no time for his companion. The dog wanted his feelings known, and the woman's question was answered.

You might hear words or see pictures. Pictures may be clear or may come through like puzzle messages that have to be pieced together. (If you read *Birdsong, Barks, and Banter*, you know about these kinds of messages.)

Sometimes, you will empathically feel a certain region of the pet is not right. When I was holding sessions at my office, I remember a young man and his dog came in for Reiki. The dog had a mysterious ailment that the vet was having a hard time diagnosing. I felt a strangeness in the dog's ear but didn't mention it, thinking this could have nothing to do with the issues in another region of his system. A couple of weeks and a couple of vets later, the young man came back to my office. He said the latest vet was able to make a diagnosis by a certain condition in the dog's ear. I didn't say anything, but boy I wished I had said something earlier.

Start with easy questions. Try something like, "What treats do you like?" A veterinarian once came to my office with her tiny dog. She was accepting of Reiki, but she was having a hard time believing in animal communication. She dared me to ask what her little dog's favorite treat was. Now, being that she was a vet, you would suppose it to be a very healthy choice. But no, a picture of a hot dog came to my mind. This little dog was telling me she loved hot dogs. For a moment, I hesitated. A vet's dog eating hot dogs? Then I told her. She gasped and said she bought those little baby jar meat sticks that look like tiny hot dogs for her dog all the time. She gobbled them up! (Later on in the session, I described the dog's favorite toy exactly to the vet. I think I opened a closed mind that evening.)

There have been times when I have felt that a client's dog or cat was close to crossing, but I never divulged this information. Why take away any moments of joy together and replace them with worry? I never give out this information. Even when I have been asked to help in the search for lost pets, I always try to ease the coming news for the owners. If I feel a pet has crossed into spirit, I usually say I feel a very weakened energy. I try to prepare their hearts, but I won't ever say anything to break them. They will be broken soon enough.

If your pet doesn't seem interested, try another time. Just like us, they have times when they don't want to be bothered. We all need our space. Don't keep forcing a pet to communicate if he or she doesn't seem to want to. Some pets, just like people, are talkers, and some are not. If your pet has an extroverted and friendly disposition, he/she will most likely be a talker. If he/she is quiet and shy, he/she may not wish to share in this type of conversation with you. Accept and love what is.

When you begin each session, ask the pet for permission to communicate. Then, focus on opening your heart chakra (if you are trying to send messages to him/her) or try to imagine his/her heart chakra opening (if you are waiting for him/her to send you an answer). You can do this most easily by envisioning a calming pink link moving from your heart to his/hers. When each session is finished, always thank your pet and praise his/her open heartedness.

Pet Auras

Pets have auras just as people do. With practice, you may begin to feel very subtle changes in the auras of your pets and detect the beginnings of any changes to their well-being.

Slowly move your hand gracefully and smoothly several inches away from your pet's body.

(Side note: The aura of a person may be several inches to several feet outside the body. I am a Reiki Master and intuitive, but I cannot have Reiki done by another practitioner touching my body directly; the energy feels too intense. When I took Reiki classes, the teacher did Reiki to my body as I lay on the table with my eyes shut. I told her she was pressing too hard; it felt very uncomfortable. She asked me if I was an intuitive, then she told me to open my eyes. Her hand was at least a foot away from my body! All the other students witnessed this fact, and I have had similar experiences with others trying to touch me directly. Another time, when I was just a beginning Reiki pupil, we practiced reading the aura of another. The teacher asked us where we felt a change in the energy. I didn't respond because I was feeling changes everywhere. I thought I was wrong. As it turned out, the teacher purposely chose this man because he was like the bionic patient; he had issues and repairs everywhere. Once you have had surgery, there is not only an opening to your physical body, but there is also a tear in your aura. Energy workers learn ways to seal these tears and strengthen your aura. You can envision tears being mended on your own pet's aura after surgery, as well as on your own body.)

Only attempt to read a pet's aura in a quiet environment; the changes are subtle and not easily felt in the beginning. If you notice a change in the energy, this might be an area where emotional or physical issues should be addressed. As I said at the beginning of this book, everyone has the ability to channel energy, some more than others. You need not study Reiki and learn proper techniques and symbols, though doing so will intensify your natural ability. Don't panic if you feel something in your pet's aura. It might be just a tummy ache or strain from overplaying. But in learning to feel auras, you can keep watch over any areas that seem different and promptly seek veterinary help if an issue escalates.

Is Animal Communication Dangerous?

Can you absorb pain and emotional trauma from animals? As a Reiki Master, there have been times (though thankfully few) when I have done Reiki on an individual suffering from a particular pain (shoulder pain, for example) and subsequently felt this pain. It was short lived; energy workers study ways to cleanse and clear their own energy fields for this purpose. In all the times I have communicated with animals, my heart has felt the sorrow of some and been deeply affected by it, but no actual pain has ever been carried across to my own energy. If you are extremely empathic, it would be wise to study energy work and learn ways to cleanse your own.

Learning Meditation

I want you to read this chapter over several times until you fully understand the meditative process. Then, practice it. It will take some effort before you are able to clear your mind and begin the communication techniques. Always try to ground yourself before doing any communication work.

Find a quiet place where you can be comfortable. Take notice of your surroundings. For example, if you are in a comfy chair, feel its plushness. If you are on your bed, feel the bedspread beneath you.

Now I want you to take a few deep breaths. It is amazing how a few deep breaths can bring you relaxation.

Next, I want you to close your eyes and imagine your perfect location. If you love the ocean, imagine walking on the beach. If you love forests, imagine walking through the woodlands. I want you to imagine that you can look upon your body and see yourself walking wherever you may wish.

Now, I want you to imagine you are not your physical being, but rather a being of light walking on that path. It is easier for some at first, but with practice, I promise it will become easier.

I want you to step back into yourself and imagine walking for a few more minutes, focusing on your breathing as you walk. Find a quiet place to sit. If at the beach, sit on the sand and watch the waves. If in the forest, find a large rock upon which to rest.

Imagine the daylight is leaving and night is descending around you. Look up at the stars as they peek through the curtain of nightfall. Find the bright North Star.

Imagine you have a tiny doorway at the top of your head. This is your intuitive doorway. Like any door, it opens a pathway for something or someone to enter. Open it and let the beams of that North Star flow within you. Send this white light into your crown chakra area, strengthening it.

Take a few deep breaths.

Starting at your head...........imagine the light swirling around your face, behind your eyes, between your ears, inside your cheekbones.

Now send the light into your neck, filling up the space with light and letting all tension leave.

Let the light flow into your upper chest and down your arms, into your wrists, and into each fingertip.

Let it swirl throughout your chest and around to your upper back.

Send it to your stomach, into your lower back and thighs, then down into each leg, calf, and foot.

Now, imagine that light flowing straight down into the earth beneath you, connecting and grounding your energy. Take a few deep breaths here. Then, look up and change the North Star to a beautiful violet beam.

Send that beam into your third eye chakra. As you do so, say these words: *Let my intuition flow freely. Let my belief in the connection and communication of all beings shine within.* Imagine the space inside your third eye chakra glowing with violet light.

Again, take a few breaths.

Now, look upon the North Star. See its color change to a beautiful blue. Send those blue beams inside through your intuitive doorway, into your jaw, within your neck and say these words: *Let my throat chakra strengthen, and let my ability to communicate with all beings shine within.*

Take a moment to breathe and imagine these colors within you.

Now, look up to the North Star and imagine that its beams have become pink. Send this loving light into your intuitive doorway and straight into your heart. Say the following: *Let my heart open to receive thoughts, and let my heart open to send thoughts to others.* Imagine your lungs filling with pink light, your heart surrounded with it. Again, breathe. Send this breath all the way into your arms, and let it fill your hands and fingers.

Now, look up again to the North Star, this time beaming with a brilliant yellow glow. Let this beam travel from the top of your head down into your intuitive gut. Take several breaths and say these words: *I have the confidence to communicate.*

Now, look upon the North Star glowing orange and send these beams into your sacral chakra. Take several breaths and say:

Let my passion for animal communication be fueled within this chakra.

Now, look again upon the Star, a brilliant red in the sky. Send its beam all the way down your body into your root chakra. Take several deep breaths, reciting these words: *I release all fear.*

Take a few breaths, then imagine you can step outside and look upon yourself once again. Imagine you are your own rainbow, each chakra shining brightly.

Now, glance upward to the North Star, beaming brightly white again. Let this white light once again flow through your body as it combines all the chakra regions into one glowing being of brilliant white light.

Step back inside your body of light and slowly begin to feel your ground, whether it be the chair you are sitting in or the bed you are lying on. Slowly open your eyes, ready to begin your communication session.

With continued meditation, you will begin to see your sleep patterns and overall wellness improve—just a few additional gifts that animal communication brings.

Once you have thanked your pet at the end of your communication session, I want you to take a moment to close your eyes, envision your light being, and close the door at the very top of your crown chakra. Closing this door at the end of any communication session protects you, just as locking your front door protects you. If you at any time feel uncomfortable doing any communication session, surround yourself with healing light.

Practicing with Friends

Have fun with these techniques. Practice them on human friends. Have a friend think of an image in his/her mind as you try to receive that image in yours. Picture the image floating on a beam of pink light as it travels from his/her heart into yours.

Have a friend focus on an emotion in his/her life. The emotion can be one of happiness or sorrow. Use your intuitive third eye to see into his/her heart and empathize.

There is such a thing as "cold readings" in the intuitive world. This entails holding an object and communicating the residual energy left within it. You can try holding a pet's collar or special toy and concentrating on whatever images come to mind. You can hold a special piece of jewelry or some object a friend uses every day, like a set of keys, and see what pictures emerge. You might be surprised at just how intuitive you are. The pupils in my workshops always were. Here, the degree of each individual's ability shone through. Some had uncanny results the very first time, but all showed some degree of natural intuitiveness.

Once, a client who had just lost her therapy dog brought his collar and leash to my office. I felt them and told her what I perceived, having known little about her personally. I asked her if she wrote; she indeed was keeping a journal of her grief. Then, I told her I saw a large, white dog coming. She was quiet in the office, but she later emailed me a picture of a beautiful, white bulldog named Diamond who would take up the reins of her beloved boy. She had been in the process of adopting Diamond when she came to my office that day.

Objects can hold a lot of their owners' energy within them. If you shop at a lot of garage sales or flea markets, pick up an object first before you buy it and try to feel its story. If disturbing emotions come to mind, perhaps it is best to pass up that particular find. There are also ways to cleanse and clear objects. On your path to learning more about energy, you will discover these ways.

Building Your Confidence

No one is perfect, and no one is right all of the time. I still doubt what comes in during communications and question gifts that I, myself, don't fully comprehend. I feel blessed to be able to help others, but I still don't fully understand how or why I was chosen to do so.

There were times when I was first scheduling sessions that I kept half of what I perceived to myself. And most times, the messages I kept hidden were the meaningful ones. One time, a dying, paralyzed dog communicated how much she enjoyed playing in the leaves recently. I said to myself, "How is this possible?" and kept my mouth shut. When the client left my office with her dog in her arms, she told me she had carried the dog outside in a huge pile of leaves (her favorite play place) and let her sit among them. I kept silent; it was too late. Would the woman have believed me, or would she have thought I just repeated what she said? If I had had the confidence not to question this message, just imagine how happy that woman would have felt, knowing the happiness she brought to her beloved dog's final days. My doubtful silence is louder than all the messages I have received throughout the years.

Relay what you perceive, even if it seems to make no sense. It might be the very thing that makes all the difference to a person whose heart is grieving.

Personalities

You will love sensing the unique personalities of each animal. You will feel the devotion of some who suffered much longer than they should have in order to remain by a loved one's side. You will pick up the mischievous sides to some who apologize for all the hijinks they caused during life. You will feel the hearts inside of them, the hearts that miss being with the ones they love. I remember all those I have communicated with and have loved each one for the furry person he or she was.

Do Pets Come Back?

After queries about the Rainbow Bridge, this has to be the most frequent question asked of me. During some communication sessions, I do pick up messages of returning. This, to me, is an animal whose spirit will come back in physical form. Not all return; some wait until energies reunite in spirit. For those that do return, a lucky few find them again. A certain puppy or kitten that mimics all that encompassed the one they lost. These finds are treasures and do not happen very often. Some pets return in physical form but share their lives with other families.

I believe all pets in energy can visit their human companions. Some come in dreams. Some come in shadows flitting across the room, or the pressure of a whiskered face brushing across the legs of a loved one. Some momentarily step within another pet and relay a message of love. Skippy was a treasured friend of mine. He was a tiny, silver poodle who always got his hunger or thirst message across by tossing his bowl across the kitchen floor. When I adopted Little Guy, an elderly pomeranian, he walked inside the house and strolled into the kitchen. We heard the familiar sound of a bowl being tossed across the floor. "It's Skippy," we all thought. And I believe it was, giving his approval. Little Guy became another treasure in my life.

The greatest gift a loved one can give to a pet that has crossed is acceptance. Accept his/her departure and tell him/her it is okay. Just like human spirits, animal spirits cannot be at peace if those left behind are overwhelmed with sadness. Don't feel like bringing home another is replacing him/her; bringing home another is bringing peace to the one who waits. But don't compare. Grieving hearts get caught up in comparing a new companion to the one who has crossed. Each one will be unique and loved in his or her own special way.

Epilogue

I hope this book has paved a path for you, hopefully the beginnings of animal communication. Animals have hearts and souls. I know; they have spoken to me. Perhaps, with practice, they will speak to you as well.

Don't get discouraged, don't lose faith, and don't feel like a failure if you cannot become an animal communicator. Whether you realize it or not, you are communicating every minute of every day with your pets. They look into our eyes and hearts as well as hear our voices each day. They feel what you are feeling. They know sadness and grief. They know the joy of your presence before you turn into your street after work each night and wait at the door, tail wagging. How do they know these things? How can they sense a vet visit is impending and hide under the bed before you even reach for the leash? How do they know that Johnny's school bus is turning down the block five minutes before you see it? Some things are real, even if you cannot see them, feel them, or write an explanation on paper.

For me, animal communication is one of these things. There are so many wondrous things in our Universe if you keep an open mind and heart to them.

May this book be your beginning.

Blessed Journey,
Shirl

Review

Let's go over all the basic steps of animal communication once more:

- First, find a quiet place.
- Start off with a photograph before you attempt face-to-snout communication.
- Begin with deep breaths and meditation to open your intuitive pathway. With practice, you will be able to clear your mind more quickly, and your meditation need not be so involved.......unless you enjoy it.
- Ask your pet's permission.
- Focus on a thought received. Always trust your first thought; ones that follow might be creations of your own imagination.
- When you are confident with thought transmissions, ask a question. Start with an easy one like, "What treats do you like most?"
- Do not get anxious if nothing comes. Your pet will pick up on that anxiousness and look upon any further communication as a stressful event.
- Be patient. This takes time, years of living with and communicating with animals.

- Always thank your pet when he/she seems disinterested. He/she may get up and walk away. Let him/her. Wait a day or two before you try again. Let this be an enjoyable experience for both of you.
- Remember to close your intuitive pathway.

I have included a little journal at the end of this book to keep all your session results in one convenient place. Keep it in the room/area where you will be attempting communication and jot down thoughts and answers as they come.

Good Luck!

Session _____ Date _____

Session _____ Date _____

Session _____ Date _____

Session _____ Date _____

Session _____   Date _____

Session _____   Date _____

Session _____   Date _____

Session _____   Date _____

Session _____   Date _____

Session _____ Date _____

www.ingramcontent.com/pod-product-compliance
Lightning Source LLC
Chambersburg PA
CBHW031453040426
42444CB00007B/1088